Consultant, Istar Schwager, holds a Ph.D. in educational psychology
and a master's degree in early childhood education.
She has been an advisor, consultant, and content designer for numerous parenting,
child development, and early learning programs including the *Sesame Street*
television show and magazines.
She has been a consultant for several Fortune 500 companies
and has regularly published articles for parents
on a range of topics.

Louis Weber, C.E.O.
Publications International, Ltd.
7373 North Cicero Avenue
Lincolnwood, Illinois 60646

Manufactured in the U.S.A.

8 7 6 5 4 3 2

ISBN 1-56173-482-9

active minds

colors

PHOTOGRAPHY
George Siede and Donna Preis

CONSULTANT
Istar Schwager, Ph.D.

Publications
International,
Ltd.

yellow

A lemon and
a slick raincoat,

Bananas and
two ducks that float.

orange

Oranges,
flowers in a vase,

Carrots,
        and a pumpkin face.

red

A fire truck, an apple,
fresh-picked cherries,

A toy ladybug,
    and ripe strawberries.

purple

Bubble gum and
a coat to wear,

A flower and
a friendly bear.

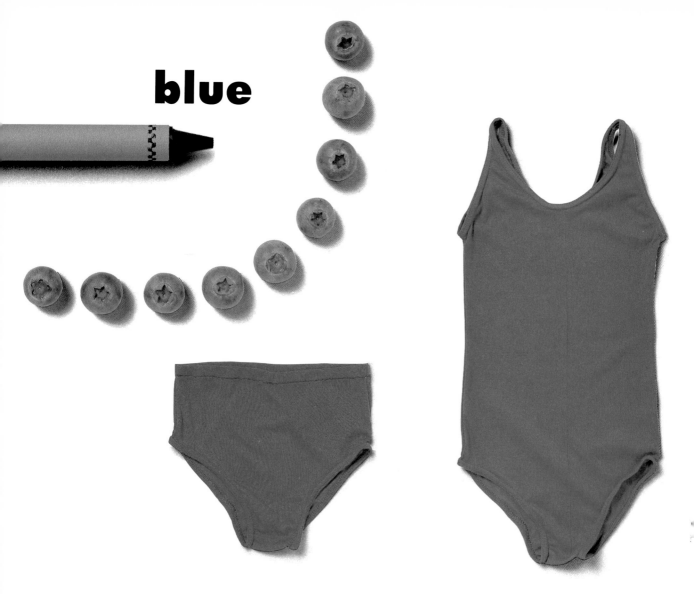

blue

Big blueberries
and bathing suits,

A pair of jeans
and new rain boots.

green

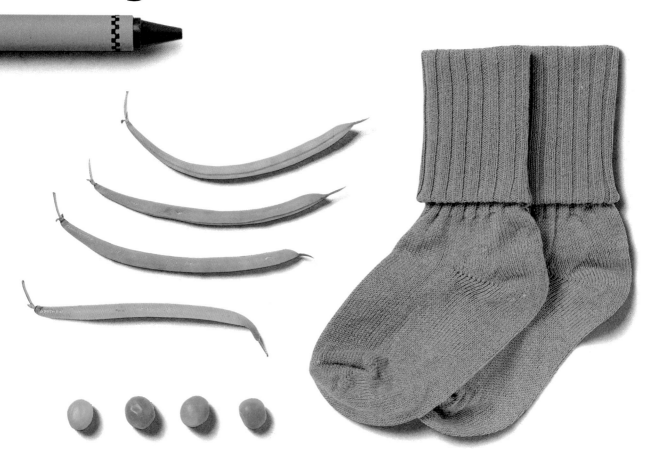

Green beans and peas,
a pair of socks,

Lunch for a turtle
in its box.

brown

A playful puppy,
a round pancake,

Peanut-butter cookies
you can bake.

black and white

A frozen snowball,
a Halloween cat,

A baby bunny,
and a magic hat.